Rob

1676 – 1745

by David Yaxley

The Larks Press
Pocket biographies No. 2

Published by the Larks Press
Ordnance Farmhouse
Guist Bottom, Dereham, Norfolk
NR20 5PF

01328 829207

British Library Cataloguing-in-Publication Data
A catalogue record for this book is available from
the British Library.

Front Cover:
Sir Robert Walpole
An engraving made in 1788 by James Watson after
Jean Baptiste Vanloo's portrait of c. 1738-40

First printed by the Larks Press in 1995

Printed by the Lanceni Press 2005

© David Yaxley 1995

ISBN 0 948400 29 3

SIR ROBERT WALPOLE

1676-1745

Of the 19 children born between 1672 and 1695 to Colonel Robert and Maria Walpole of Houghton, only four boys and three girls survived to adulthood. The eldest son, Edward, was named after his grandfather, the first Walpole for ten generations to be knighted. The second surviving son, born in 1676, was named Robert after his father, and the third, born in 1678, was called Horatio. Houghton and Raynham, seat of Horatio, the 1st Viscount Townshend, were only 7 miles apart; Colonel Robert often visited Raynham, and was named as an executor in Lord Townshend's will. At the age of six, Robert Walpole joined Edward at the Revd Richard Ransome's school at Great Dunham, 11 miles from Houghton, returning home only a few times a year. In 1690 Robert followed Charles, 2nd Viscount Townshend to Eton. They were to remain friends and colleagues for nearly 40 years.

The Walpole family came from Walpole in west Norfolk, but from before 1286 they had held land in Houghton, their main seat after about 1310. The Townshends had acquired land in Raynham only just before 1400, but whereas the Walpoles had mostly remained untitled country gentry, the Townshends had four generations of knights in the 16th century and had received a baronetcy in 1682. This was the basis for Charles Townshend's assumption of social superiority over Robert Walpole.

In 1696 Robert followed his brother and Charles Townshend to King's College Cambridge, but on Edward's death in 1698 he was summoned back to Houghton. His father was in poor health and needed help to run the estate, which then amounted to over 11,000 acres in six villages, plus property in Suffolk. On 30th July 1700 Robert married Catherine Shorter, who brought a dowry of £7,000 from her father, a Baltic timber merchant. She was beautiful, with sensuous lips, enormous dark eyes and a fine figure, but she was subject to uncontrollable fits of jealousy and anger. Her London upbringing with her giddy grandmother, Lady Philipps, gave her an insatiable appetite for fashion and extravagance, and after the first few passionate years, their married life was unhappy and increasingly disjointed.

Colonel Robert died on November 18th 1700, his fiftieth birthday, and Robert succeeded to the estate. His income from land and rents was about

£2,000 a year, but as well as his own household he had to keep his mother, two younger brothers and two sisters and pay two life annuities. He entered politics immediately, succeeding his father in January 1701 as one of the two M.P.s for Castle Rising. In 1702, because of family pressure, he switched to King's Lynn, which he represented as a Whig until 1742. He was tall and well-built, (later he became enormous) and could dominate company by his physical presence. His conversation was open, sharp, witty and sometimes coarse, with, according to Pope, 'the horse-laugh'. Like his brother Horatio, he never lost his Norfolk accent. In Parliament he proved a good speaker and a brilliant debater with a prodigious memory for facts and a supreme gift for marshalling arguments.

Robert and Catherine set up house in Dover Street, London. His political influence in Norfolk was useful to the Whigs, but it was his character, ability, and influential friends, including Lord Orford, Lord Godolphin and the Duke and Duchess of Marlborough, that enabled him to rise swiftly. In 1705 he became a member of Prince George's Admiralty Council, where his skill in rationalising the tangled finances of the navy made him virtual leader of that Council. Political realignments soon led to the inclusion of more

Whigs in the government, and in 1708 Walpole became Secretary-at-War, in control of recruitment, promotions and supplies in Great Britain. In 1710 he became also Treasurer of the Navy. As well as a salary, both offices brought opportunities for legal profits on the side. Townshend, meanwhile, was occupied in continental diplomacy.

The general election of 1710, which brought the Tories under Harley to office, led to the dismissal of Walpole as Secretary-at-War, and in 1711 he lost the Treasureship of the Navy. Out of office, he became one of the leaders of the opposition, and in 1712, in a Tory drive to prove that the Whigs had prolonged the French wars for private gain, he and Marlborough were accused of corruption. Walpole was charged with receiving money from forage contractors, particularly his friend and banker, Robert Mann; this was untrue, but the Tory Commons found him guilty, expelled him from the House and committed him to the Tower. Nonetheless the bye-election at Lynn returned him unopposed, and when the Commons refused to accept the result the extreme Whig, John Turner, was elected.

Released from the Tower, Walpole was again returned for Lynn in the general election of 1713, and in July the recently widowed Lord Townshend married Dorothy, Robert's enchanting and impetuous favourite sister. Queen Anne was dying, and Walpole's arch-enemy Bolingbroke hoped that James Stuart, the Old Pretender, could be persuaded to renounce his Roman Catholicism and succeed to the throne. Walpole warned the Commons in the strongest terms that the Protestant succession, in the person of George, Elector of Hanover, was in danger. In the event, the Pretender refused to change his religion, the Queen dismissed Harley (Lord Oxford), and did not promote Bolingbroke. The Hanoverian succession was assured and with it the dominance of the Whigs.

Anne died on August 1st 1714. In the new government of George I, Townshend became Secretary of State for the North and Walpole Paymaster-General, a lucrative post which he may have chosen to pay off his mounting debts. In the next three years £109,208, of which he invested £61,778, passed through his hands. Much of the rest was spent on the lavish hospitality expected of a leading politician. He took over Orford House at Chelsea Hospital, where he appointed Robert Mann Deputy-Treasurer, and the Rector of Great Bircham, Henry Bland, Chaplain. He moved from Dover Street to a bigger house in Arlington Street which he used virtually as his political headquarters.

He now had four children: Robert (born 1701), Catherine (1703), Mary (1704) and Edward (1706). Although he and Catherine lived together, their relations were strained and both were having casual affairs.

The Tories were in disarray. Oxford had been sent to the Tower and Bolingbroke had fled to the Pretender in France. In September 1715 the Jacobite rebellion, aimed at putting the Pretender on the throne, broke out in Scotland. Form measures by Townshend and Stanhope, Secretaries of State, prevented any support developing in England, and the Scottish rebellion petered out after the indecisive battle of Sheriffmuir. Meanwhile Walpole had succeeded Lord Halifax as Chancellor of the Exchequer and First Lord of the Treasury, head of the Board that had replaced the ancient office of Treasurer. The government was purged of all Jacobites and Tories, but immediately the Whigs developed factions. Stanhope and Sunderland, with George I in Hanover, began the process of reversing British policy by negotiating an alliance with France, part of George's plan to protect his beloved Hanover. The protests of Walpole and Townshend at this *volte-face* were of no avail, and early in 1717 Townshend was deprived of his office and offered the Lord-Lieutenancy of Ireland. He grudgingly accepted, only to be deprived of the new post a couple of months later. Walpole and others resigned in protest.

Out of office for the next three years, Walpole and Townshend were the leaders of the Whig opposition to the ministry of Stanhope and Sunderland. During this period Walpole got to know Prince George, later Gorge II, and Princess Caroline, with whom he soon developed a bond of mutual admiration. He also found time to attend to his Norfolk estate. Further improvements to the old house were carried out, major woods were planted, and the great semi-formal garden west of the house was completed. Thomas Badeslade made excellent surveys and estate maps which are still at Houghton. In 1717 Horace, the last of Catherine's children was born. Contemporary rumour credited the child to Lord Hervey; however, Walpole acknowledged the child, and Horace, who worshipped his mother, always referred to Walpole as his father.

In 1719, after Walpole had shown his strength in opposition by engineering the defeat of Stanhope's Peerage Bill, the ministry sought a reconciliation. Townshend was appointed Lord President of the Council in 1720 and Walpole again became Paymaster-General. Much of the profit from Walpole's years in office had been invested in the East India and South Sea Companies. Stock of the latter company, founded in 1711 with a monopoly of the South Sea trade, rose enormously in value when it outbid the Bank of England in a scheme to take over the National Debt. Walpole, doubtful of the scheme's viability, had sold all his South Sea stock by March 1720 and re-invested the proceeds elsewhere, but in June he bought £9,000 of South Sea stock at its peak value, and was only prevented from buying more by the sagacity of his banker Robert Jacombe. A sudden massive loss of public confidence led, in September, to the bursting of the 'South Sea Bubble', bringing financial ruin to some M.P.s and ministers, including the Chancellor of the Exchequer, Aislabie, who was sent to the Tower.

Walpole had gone to Norfolk at the height of the fever speculation. When the crash came, except for one brief visit, he cannily stayed away from London, until the clamour for his return to clear up the mess became irresistible. Back in London he persuaded Parliament to accept a plan, largely the work of Jacombe, to transfer South Sea stock to the Bank of England and the East India Company. No one was enthusiastic, but Walpole's calmness and persistence led to a slow return of confidence. The death of Stanhope in 1721 brought a reconstruction of the ministry. Sunderland, acquitted on a bribery charge largely through Walpole's efforts, remained in the ministry and his office as Groom of the Stole gave him the ear of the King and a seat in the Cabinet. Townshend and Lord Carteret became the Secretaries of State and Walpole resumed the offices of Chancellor of the Exchequer and First Lord of the Treasury.

The next few months were crowded. In a damage limitation exercise Walpole averted the full prosecution of the South Sea directors and saved most of the estate of Aislabie from forfeiture, earning himself the title of 'Skreen Master General'. He took steps, unpopular at the time, to ensure the future stability of the Company, partly by writing off £4 million of its debt. The death of Sunderland in 1722 removed his main rival, and for the next few years he and Townshend jointly dominated the ministry.

However politics was not Walpole's only interest. The old house at Houghton was at best a patchwork, incorporating work from the 15th to the 17th century. The steward, James Rolfe, wrote in June 1721: 'I am writing this in yor Honours Study where I have a thousand ungrateful Companions of the Mice; who doe dayly despoile to yore papers parchments & Bookes...the vermin have nibbled holes and made Free passages in to the drawers, they run in such numbers 'tis impossible to think of destroying them unless the whole be removed'. A week later Walpole replied, 'I have advised my Sister Hamond [Susan, wife of Anthony Hamond of Wootton] to goe to Houghton to call a Council of War about the Mice, if they cannot be conquer'd or drove away...we must remove the books'. However, he had already decided, nearly a year before, to build a grand new house.

Between April and September 1720 Walpole bought more estates in Norfolk, including Crostwight for £21,000 and there were rumours in London that he was about to receive a peerage. In fact he remained a commoner until 1742, but the possibility of having to support the dignity of a peerage may have been one reason why he decided to enlarge his estate and build a new house.

In the total absence of hard evidence to support the recent speculation that James Gibbs designed Houghton, its attribution to Colen Campbell must stand. Campbell was the leading exponent of the Neo-Palladian style, and his responsibility for Houghton was accepted without question at the time. Thomas Ripley, a carpenter-turned-architect, was appointed supervisor of the work, and in June

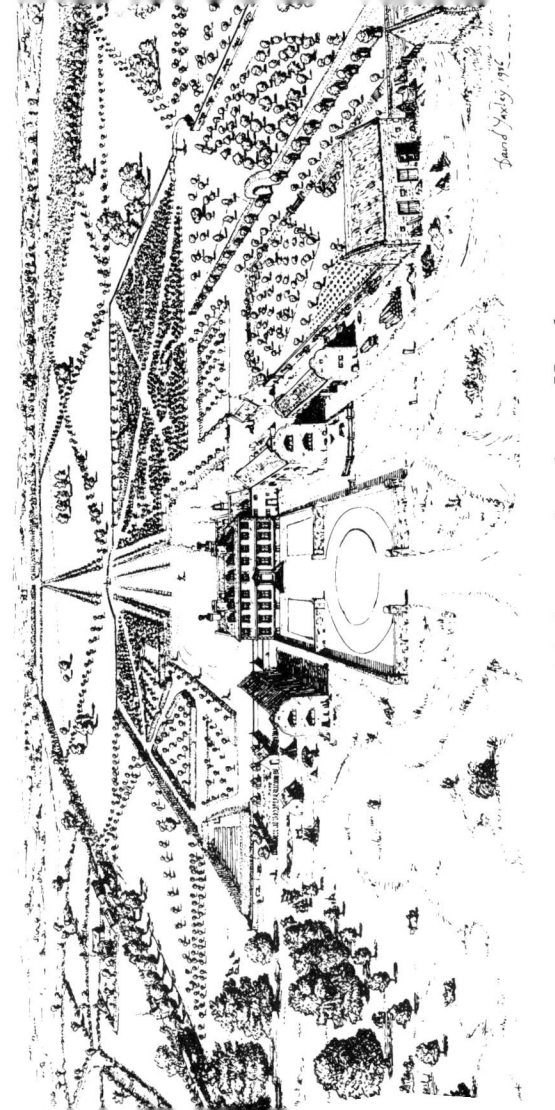

A reconstruction of the house and gardens at Houghton in about 1720

1721 went to Yorkshire for suitable stone for the exterior of the house, making an advantageous deal for the beautiful Jurassic sandstone from a quarry near Whitby. The stone was to be used only on the surfaces; millions of local bricks formed the core of the building. The foundation stone of the house, immediately eats of the old hall was laid on 24th May 1722. By 1725 the south-west tower was complete, and by 1726 William Kent was working on designs for furniture and decoration. Money flowed freely; a rare surviving monthly account shows £2,693 14s. 8d was spent in July 1726. By 1728 the structural work was nearly complete and, despite a fire in 1732, the house was declared finished in 1735. The park was enlarged and planted; a Palladian water-tower, a magnificent stable-block, and a new tower for the church were built. The old village, too close to the mansion, was demolished, and a new one, complete with model farm and inn, was developed outside the park.

The first great test of the Walpole-Townshend ministry came in 1722, when a ramshackle Jacobite plot, centred on Francis Atterbury, the brilliant, violent and ambitious Bishop of Rochester, was uncovered. Proof of Atterbury's treason was unobtainable, and he was merely banished; other plotters were imprisoned and the only one executed was

Christopher Layer, an unsuccessful Norfolk lawyer daft enough to commit his wild plans to paper. The ruthless exposure of the plotters, and Walpole's development of a network of continental spies, effectively suppressed the Jacobite menace for the rest of the ministry. Walpole's identification of Tories with Jacobitism made an alliance between Tories and dissonant Whigs unlikely. The supremacy of Walpole and Townshend was assured when, in 1723, Carteret, their strongest rival, was forced to resign. He was replaced by the compliant Duke of Newcastle, who had extensive electoral patronage. Growing control of all kinds of patronage and of parliamentary business provided a firm base for Walpole's aim of peace and prosperity. His political success was marked by the creation of the Barony of Walpole of Walpole for his son Robert (1723), and his own knighthoods of the Bath (1725) and the Garter (1726).

In 1724 Walpole fell in love with a beautiful and lively Irish girl, Maria Skerret, who became his mistress and later his wife. She bore him a daughter, Maria, in 1725, and with them he found a family happiness lacking in his marriage. At about the same time his daughter Mary married George Cholmondeley, Viscount Malpas; their grandson would inherit Houghton in 1797. In the same period came three personal bereavements. In 1722, his daughter Catherine died after a long illness and in 1726 his beloved younger brother, Galfridus, also died. A politically more important death was that of his sister Dorothy Townshend; she was a strong personal link between the two leaders, and her death in 1726 preceded a deterioration in their relations.

In 1727 George I died. It was by no means certain that Walpole would remain chief minister, but after a half-hearted attempt to promote Spencer Compton, George II was persuaded by Queen Caroline, and by the ease with which Walpole secured a greatly increased Civil List from the Commons, that it as best to continue the existing ministry. Its policy since 1721 had been to keep Britain out of wars and to protect and increase her trade particularly with Spanish possessions in America. This led to a succession of treaties and shifting alliances; with Horatio, Walpole's brother, in the Paris embassy, Townshend concentrated on the alliance with France, but from about 1727 French and British interests began to diverge. Walpole saw Spain as the main threat to trade and the Austrian Emperor as our natural ally, and pressed this point of view. Townshend, arrogant and inflexible, became increasingly isolated in his

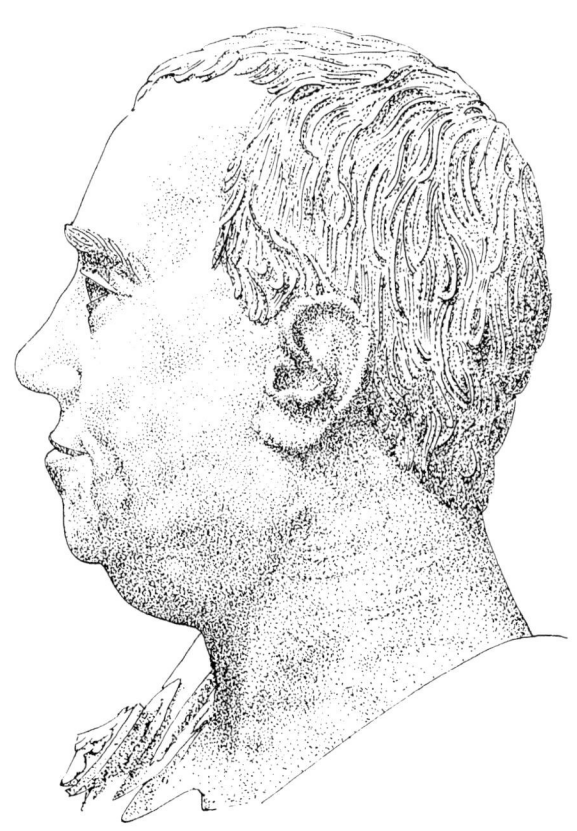

Sir Robert Walpole
Drawing by David Yaxley after a bust by John Michael Rysbrack
c. 1730

support of France and in 1730 he resigned. In a reshuffled ministry Walpole directed foreign affairs through his Secretaries of State, Newcastle and Lord Harrington, and the speedy conclusion of a treaty with Austria completed the reversal of Townshend's policies.

Walpole's friendship with the King and Queen prevented conflict between national policy and Court interests, but it was his skilful management of Parliament that maintained him in power for 12 years after Townshend's resignation. His period of office strengthened the Commons enormously against the Lords, the Court, and all outside influences, and ensured that the King's communication with the government should always be through the head of the ministry. However, he still sometimes had to rely on the Whig majority in the Lords to block opposition bills. His only real failure before 1739 was the sensible attempt, in 1733, to transfer the duties on tobacco and wine from customs to excise; this would have hit smuggling, increased revenue, and ensured that towns and the business community, which Walpole hated, were taxed on a scale similar to that of the Land Tax, paid mainly by the country gentry. He dropped the scheme when he realised that the public, fearing a universal excise enforced by an army of excisemen, was putting unbearable pressure on his Whig M.P.s. Perhaps unwisely he dismissed from their places many who had temporarily deserted him. The general election of 1734 saw his majority drop to about 100, but although he was reasonably sure of another full term of seven years, new M.P.s like William Pitt, George Lyttleton, and Richard Grenville formed the core of an effective new opposition. The Duke of Argyll, who controlled many Scottish seats, was antagonised and the court of the Prince of Wales, who was indignant at Walpole's refusal to increase his allowance, became the centre of opposition.

In spite of this, Sir Robert must still have appeared all-powerful. Even before Houghton was complete he had begun to use it for the famous 'Houghton Congress' meetings of friends and political colleagues. According to Lord Hervey, the rustic or ground floor was 'dedicated to fox-hunters, noise, dirt and business'. They sat down to dinner 'a little snug party of about thirty odd, up to the chin in beef, venison, geese, turkey etc.; and generally over the chin in claret, strong beer, and punch. We had Lords spiritual and temporal, besides commoners, parsons and freeholders innumerable. In public we drank loyal healths, talked of the times and cultivated popularity: in private we drew plans and cultivated the Country'. For Horace Walpole, first visiting the new house in

Horace Walpole at the age of 10
Engraving by S.Smith

1736, it was a revelation to see his father so genial and friendly, and he was entranced by the house and the pictures.

Walpole had begun to collect paintings in about 1717, and using friends, relatives, agents, and diplomats he assembled a magnificent collection. The catalogue of 1747 lists 221 paintings in the main rooms. His favourite painters were the Italians of the 17th and early 18th centuries, of whose work he had 69 examples, including 13 by Carlo Maratti. There was a Holy Family and 13 portraits by Vandyke, 23 landscapes, 17 genre paintings, and a few sporting, animal and still life subjects. In 1779 the bulk of the collection was sold by Sir Robert's grandson to Catherine of Russia.

Catherine Walpole died in August 1737, and, soon after, Walpole married Maria Skerret; but she died in childbirth in June 1738 and was buried alongside her predecessor at Houghton. Queen Caroline died in August 1737. These blows, coming with bouts of ill-health, brought uncharacteristic melancholy and depression which remained with Sir Robert, with only brief intervals, for the rest of his life. Worsening relations with Spain forced him, in 1739, to yield to public clamour and declare war. Walpole was not optimistic: 'They now ring the bells, they will soon wring their hands.' He was an administrator who worked best in peacetime, and would perhaps have preferred to resign. A motion on the pre-war negotiations with Spain became a personal vote of confidence, and this encouraged the opposition in January 1741 to move a vote of censure, claiming that Walpole had acted unconstitutionally in making himself 'sole minister' and, by implication, 'prime minister' invading the responsibilities of his colleagues. Walpole made a brilliant speech, and the Tories, with many of whom he was personally

Houghton
Drawing by David Yaxley

popular, refused to vote against him. The general election of 1741 brought him a theoretical majority of 19; but the European situation drew him reluctantly into a war on Austria's behalf against

Prussia, soon to be allied with France and Spain. Newcastle and Hardwicke had conspired with his old enemies Carteret and Pulteney, and together they arranged a cynical alliance with the Tories and Jacobites. On 11th of February, 1742, after a defeat on an election petition, Walpole resigned. Two days before, he had accepted the Earldom of Orford, a title chosen in honour of his old friend Edward Russell, Earl of Orford. Pulteney was created Earl of Bath; Walpole's remark, 'My Lord Bath, you and I are now as insignificant men as any in England', was as much a statement of the changed relationship between the two Houses as a comment on personal status.

The inevitable Commons investigation into his conduct over his long ministry petered out for lack of evidence. He had made a fortune, and spent it all on living and on Houghton: at his death he had debts of £50,000. Though still consulted by the King, he spent more time at Houghton, making the final selection and arrangement of his pictures. Horace made several long visits to Houghton, getting to know and love a father for whom he had previously had merely a distant respect. In spite of the friendship of his youngest son and the delights of Houghton, there can be little doubt that, after 40 years as a leading politician, he found retirement dull. He had never been a voracious reader: he told Henry Fox, 'I totally neglected reading when I was in business and to such a degree that I cannot now read a page'; an anonymous report claimed that he 'was one day surprised in tears in his Library on his not being able after much trouble to meet about a book that suited his fancy'. By now of enormous bulk, he suffered agonies from gout and the stone.

He left Houghton for the last time in the autumn of 1744. In London, he became the victim of a violent remedy, the *Lixivium Lithontripticum*. Horace noted his last words: 'Dear Horace this Lixivium has blown me up. It has tore me to pieces. The Affair is over with me…Give me more Opium; knock me down. I expect nothing but to have ease. Dear Horace if one must die, 'tis hard to die in pain. Why do you all stand round me! Are ye all waiting there, because this is the last night…'Tis impossible not to be a little disturb'd at going out of the world, but you see I am not afraid'. He died on March 18th 1745, and was buried in Houghton church alongside his wives and his daughter.

Books about Sir Robert Walpole
Sir Robert Walpole: The Making of a Statesman
Sir Robert Walpole: The King's Minister
by J.H.Plumb
Sir Robert Walpole by B.W.Hill
Horace Walpole by R.W.Ketton-Cremer